THE FULL QUIVER

BRENNAN KOCH

Cover and Artwork by Bethany Huffman.

Dedication

This book is dedicated to my hunting partners. I love days in the field with my dad, Jon, and my two boys, Carson and Cooper.

Contents

1. September — 1
2. The Instinct — 5
3. The Flemish Bowstring — 8
4. The Anchor Point — 12
5. The Stand — 15
6. The Trail Camera — 19
7. The Meat Pack — 22
8. The Grunt — 25
9. The World's First GPS — 28
10. The Wrong End of the Binoculars — 31
11. Cut on Contact — 34
12. The Glow Stick — 37
13. The Garbage Bag Canteen — 40
14. The Range Finder — 43
15. The Nock — 46
16. The Wind Checker — 50
17. The Spine — 53
18. The Hydration Pack — 56
19. The Cover Scent — 59
20. The Messy Pack — 62
21. The Hoochie Mama — 65
22. Slave to the Safety Harness — 68
23. The Camouflage — 72
24. The First Knife — 75
25. Tuning Your Cams — 78
26. The Game Ear — 81
27. Practice, Practice, Practice — 84
28. The Small Peep — 87
29. The Fall-away Rest — 90
30. The Sharp Knife — 93
31. The Full Quiver — 96

Acknowledgments

My most pointed thanks to the Creator who so richly blesses us.

Thanks to my grandfather, Max Huffman, who was not only a model of how to walk the walk, but also a supreme editor.

Preface

This book was born out of two of my greatest passions in life; bowhunting and Jesus Christ. My hope is that as you read you will find yourself thinking back to your fond memories in the field as well as taking some valuable lessons about your spiritual walk. I want you to be able to see Christ in all things; from a bowstring to a sharp knife to the practice sessions in your back yard. My prayer is that you will grow closer to the Creator as you read stories of the great pursuit of creation.

Brennan Koch

1. September

It was the wrong answer in so many ways; yet the right answer too. Dad's answer to my loaded question of "Do you know what today is?" had been "Opening day of archery season." Innocent sounding enough to a family living in the mountain playground of McCall, Idaho. Innocent enough as long as "today" isn't your forgotten anniversary and your kid is making a bee-line to tell mom that you forgot. Yet in a way, it was the right answer. For their anniversary is the first day of September.

There is something different about waking up on the 1st of September. There is a crisp cut to the air that tells my soul that snow is coming and it's time to unleash my bottled carnivore instinct. Somehow, when the ninth month starts, my senses become more sensitive. Winds shifting as I walk through town begin to alert me. The tiny sounds of squirrels digging in my garbage can make me go into full alert. The sky up behind Lolo Peak appears to be more intense blue, but the peak seems to be looking over its shoulder for that first storm to roll out of the arctic. All

1

of a sudden, with a small change on a calendar, all those practice arrows that stuck into dirt banks or popped pinecones off low-hanging branches don't mean much as I know that my next arrow will flying toward flesh.

Even last night, as some non-hunting friends sat around a pizza, looking out the windows at March gray, I tried to explain the beauty and the magnetic attraction I have for September. The conversation started about a cell-phone call that had woke me from an early afternoon nap last September.

"What are you doing?"

"Taking a nap."

"Oh, I thought you would be out hunting today."

"I am."

The confused friend asked me where exactly I had been sleeping. In the instant that I formulated my answer, a million sensory memories blazed through my mind. The smells of the drying grasses, the hint of fall color that tinges every leaf, sounds of ravens and their awkward, throaty squawks as their wings whistle overhead. The sounds of the bulls bugling in the valley below me that had since died down as the sun came up. Even the patch of sun that I laid down in; it should have been hot, but its strength was giving way to a planet tipping on its axis away from the sun. I reflected, with that bite of pepperoni pizza in my mouth about waking up on a ridge and feeling the sense of vitality and impending death, all at the same time. My answer was less descriptive.

"Oh, up on the ridge."

"You mean in the dirt?

Yes, in the dirt, and everything else, but in the dirt all the same.

I enjoy summers. Playing with my boys, camping, fishing, picnics, all the things that make summer wonderful are of great value to me. But there is also a part of my heart that silently waits with anticipation for September. Especially through the parts of summer that are not my favorite; mowing the lawn, weeding the gardens, spraying for wasps, and sweating through sweltering heat, my mind will easily jump up onto a 7,000 foot ridge with bulls bugling in the distance. That is the anticipation of joy. It is coming, just hang on.

I can't say for sure that Jesus would have been a bow hunter should he have lived today, but I understand something of his heart; his heart of joy. Hundreds of times throughout scripture, but particularly in the New Testament, joy is promised just on the other side of a judgment or choice. Even Christ himself was faced with the concept of impending joy. "Let us fix our eyes on Jesus, the author and perfecter of our faith, who for the joy set before him endured the cross, scorning its shame and sat down at the right hand of the throne of God." (Hebrews 12:2) As I read that scripture, it becomes scarily obvious that Christ made a difficult decision. He chose to die for sinners; to absorb the ridicule and torture that was the cross so that He, and therefore I, can be in the presence of God. He knew that in the presence of the Father existed real joy. Eternal joy. Uncompromising joy. The type of complete, overwhelming, sensory perfection awaits us that beats a lifetime of Septembers in Montana.

If Christ's eyes were fixed on the joy that eternal communion with the Father would bring, then that is where my eyes belong as well. There will always be lawns to mow and wasps to spray, but my hope, my heart, and my strength will be pulling toward heaven, the best September yet.

I know I will have the right answer when I die and face the judgment washed in Christ's perfecting blood, the Father will ask me if I know what day it is. I will say, "It's the first of September."

"For what is our hope, our joy, or the crown which we will glory in the presence of our Lord Jesus when he comes?"
I Thessalonians 2:19

2. The Instinct

I love the concept of being an instinctive shooter. Seeing my target with both eyes open, feeling the strain of my longbow as I draw, reaching my anchor point and then watching as my arrow buries itself into that tiny tuft of hair right behind the shoulder of my quarry. It is a beautiful thing. The problem is that my instincts aren't that great. I am a science teacher. Everything must be calculated. Leave no extra variables in the system. Measure. Analyze. I built a longbow to help break me of my calculating ways. I love shooting it, but I find myself straining against my calculating mind.

I had the opportunity to teach a bow-building class in the small Christian school where I normally teach science. Both times I taught the class, it was a wonderful experience. I loved watching these young men toil and sweat over their precious bows. Some of them spent hour upon hour perfecting the fit and finish of the bow before ever shooting it, while others rushed through just to get to the range.

The real fascinating part of the experience happened at our little makeshift archery range. Some boys, most of whom had never shot a longbow before, picked up their bow and with a few basic pointers were sticking their arrows into pop cans at 20 yards. Others, however, could never quite wrap their mind around the concept of letting their instincts take over. The struggling guys would ask their friends how they did it. Invariably, the response was "I don't know, just shoot."

Just shoot. That is how we should live our lives in the Spirit. If we focus too long and hard on life's problems and uncertainties, we may shift our aim away from God's perfect target for our lives. I want to look at the world that God has put in front of me, listen to the Spirit, and let fly. But many times I find myself calculating. If only I had a 20-yard-life pin. I could look through my neat little peep sight, line up the glowing red pin, and accomplish what God has for me. It doesn't work that way. If we had fancy, luminescent, angle-correcting sights for our life, we wouldn't have to listen to the Spirit. Our range finder and pins would do all the work for us. God has a better plan. He wants us to rely on His quiet voice. Don't measure and calculate, but listen to the Spirit and shoot. Yes, we still need to have both eyes open, looking at the world around us, but we also must have a trusting heart.

If we spend too much effort calculating the human options and budgets for our ministry, we may not see what the Lord has for us. Lean your head away from that peep sight and take a look at the big picture of your ministry. I use the term ministry in the broadest sense of the term. God has a perfect plan for your life. And, through the

Spirit's guidance, you can follow through with that plan. For some, that may mean that your ministry is providing for your family and raising up the next generation. For others it might mean dropping everything and going into a pastorate. At a film festival just the other day, a man caught me on the way out and asked if I was "in the ministry". My answer took a second, but as my mind flashed through the science labs, basketball games, and study halls that I have experienced, it was easy to answer, "yes". Focus not on the troublesome little problems that get in our way, but look to the big picture of bettering your world for the kingdom.

Remember; look with both eyes open, focus on the eternal goal, strain your muscles to pull the load God has for you, listen to the Spirit and let it fly.

"For our light and momentary troubles are achieving for us an eternal glory that far outweighs them all. So we fix our eyes not on what is seen, but what is unseen. For what is seen is temporary, but what is unseen in eternal."
II Corinthians 4:17-18

3.   The Flemish Bowstring

It was the most dangerous weapon I have ever held in my hands. It was a crossbow, with exotic hardwoods in the stock. It had laminated wood and fiberglass limbs. And I had made it. Actually, I helped a zealous student from my longbow class make the crossbow. He had finished his longbow, and was looking for another project, so we decided to design our own crossbow. We had laminated the stock and whittled the trigger cam out of ebony. We fashioned the trigger out of a curtain rod support, which we heated with a torch and hammered into shape. The limbs were stout; at least 100 pound draw weight, and the string we had made in the Flemish style. We prayed each time that we hauled it back that the string would hold.

In fact, every time you sighted down the barrel of the weapon, somewhere in the back of your mind was that little voice reminding you that a 17-year-old had whittled the trigger cam! Yes, it was dangerous; and did it ever shoot arrows. While our 55-pound longbows were sticking arrows half way through the musty hay that we had hauled up into our range, the crossbow would drill its bolts through the hay and embed in the plywood behind. It was truly a powerful machine. And all the while, that short little bowstring held it all together.

When I taught the class to create a Flemish bowstring, one of the boys asked when we were going to learn the knot that held it together. "There is no knot," I replied to a puzzled look on his face. No, the string is just 18 strands twisting themselves back on each other. No knot. No clamps. Just twists.

I loved watching their clumsy fingers wax up a fresh set of black polyester strands. They would struggle to hold the unruly black mess tight and watched as their bowstrings unraveled into a rat's nest. Then, over time, one of them would get the feel for it. He would twist one bundle away from his body and then cross it over back toward his body. And the most amazing thing would happen; it would stay! He would do it again. And again it stayed.

Soon he had made enough cord to wrap around the string grooves in his bow, and he would double the cord back on itself. All of a sudden, the twisting, pinching, tightening and struggling would literally come full circle. A tidy little string loop lay at the end of what had originally been numerous, thin, individual black strands. He would cautiously test it, tugging at it gently, then getting more aggressive. The string stretched and twisted, but the loop held firm. It was complete. No knots needed.

This morning I looked across my church congregation and was struck by the fact that there is not a single person like me in that church. Oh, there are some young fathers, of which I am one. And some teachers, too, I suppose. There are outdoor enthusiasts. There are old ladies and people with tattoos. There are piercings and floral dresses. There are addicts and counselors. And there are sinners. And finally there is a category in which I fit in very comfortably with every other member. No, on the surface we are not alike. But yet each week I return to approximately the same pew and strive to learn more about Christ with all of the other diverse members of our church. And, much to my surprise, that is how God intended it.

Just listen to the words that Paul uses to describe the workings of the church. "There are different kinds of working, but the same God works all of them in all men." (I Corinthians 12:6) Unlike the strands of a bowstring, we are all different. But our Father has twisted us together in a powerful and useful string. There is no special knot that takes the diverse beings, who were created in God's image and locks them up together as a church. Rather, there is a singular Spirit with a singular purpose, to bring all men to God so that He might be glorified.

And so I sat in church with maybe 500 individual unruly strands, and felt the strong hand of the Spirit twist me away from his body and bring me back. And I stayed. And when He is done, the loop that He creates could never be frayed. Not even by my whittled cam.

"All of these are the work of one and the same Spirit,
and he gives them to each one, just as he
determines."
I Corinthians 12:11

4. The Anchor Point

There is a spot on my cheek, just below the cheekbone, that the knuckles from my right hand fits nicely. It is my anchor point. I learned the importance of an anchor point from the very beginning of my archery career. Even when I was just shooting light recurves as a kid, I would always come to my anchor; middle finger in the corner of my mouth. The anchor point is the heart of every good shot. The more places on your face that you can anchor your shot, the better you are. Peep sights, kisser buttons, the string on your nose, fingers touching your face all stand as little subtle reminders that yes, you are in the right spot.

It is amazing the effect that a little change in the anchor point will make. On my way to a 3-D shoot, I asked my brother-in-law if I could borrow his backup release. I was considering buying one and wanted to know how it felt. The first target was a bear on all fours facing right. I promptly put my first shot straight into the butt. Next, was a bedded elk. Stuck it in the neck, off to the left. The final straw was a huge cobra standing right in front of a massive boulder. You guessed it, a shattered arrow, off to the left. I was kicking myself for my poor display of shooting prowess, when I really began to analyze the problem. My old release allowed me to have my knuckle on my cheekbone and then the release laid along my cheek. The new release wouldn't touch my face. It was only a few millimeters of difference, but after the change was magnified down range, it resulted in a pile of busted-up carbon fibers.

In Holy Scripture we find an anchor point for each of our lives. The point is brought up over and over from Genesis to Revelation. The anchor point for our spiritual lives is a broken and contrite heart. God is less effective at directing our lives when we allow our own pride to get in the way. Isaiah says that the person God esteems is the man who is humble and contrite in spirit. He explains that God does not necessarily revel in our physical acts of worship, but what he really wants as the anchor point we should reach is the humble spirit. Isaiah offers us some perspective. "This is what the Lord says: 'Heaven is my throne, and the earth is my footstool. Where is the house you will build for me? Where will my resting place be? Has not my hand made all these things, and so they came into being' declares the Lord." (Isaiah 66:1-2) If this is truly God's footstool, what really can we offer this God? Would a 15 percent tithe be better? What if we prayed three times a day? What if we never swore again? I think you get my point. The only thing I can offer the omniscient, omnipresent, all-powerful God of the universe is something that he already made; me. The only way to lay the offering of my life on the footstool of the Lord is to break my own stubborn spirit out of reverence for a just and holy God.   When we actively seek the Lord in humbleness, he is gracious to forgive us of our sins and sends us off like an arrow flying straight and true.

What is getting in the way of your anchor point? Is it self-righteousness or God's grace that sets the course for your life?   Are your pride and your selfishness pushing that true anchor point further and further away? If so, cast off those things and watch as God puts you in that little pocket below His cheekbone; the perfect anchor point.

"This is the one I esteem: he who is humble and contrite in spirit and trembles at my word."
Isaiah 66:2

5. The Stand

I have a picture of my four-year-old son that I love. He is sitting on his knees, half-leaning over the edge of his treestand with his hands sticky from the purple sucker he is slowly devouring. We had done a practice run up a tree into a treestand, just to see if he could handle the height. We practiced tying up his rock-climbing harness and clipping it into my harness for the climb up. Like an umbilical cord, he was connected to me as we climbed up the tree steps into the stands I had hung side by side.

After only a few minutes of acclimation and half of a backpack full of food, Carson's fears were long gone and his sense of adventure took over. In his quietest hunting voice, he leaned over to my stand and asked if he could hang onto a branch above his head. Thinking that he just wanted to steady himself on his seat, I said "Yes". I was surprised to see him swing his feet off the stand while he hung on the branch like a jungle gym. It was then that three does unknowingly approaching our stand decided to bust away from the swinging monkey in the tree.

I can also picture Mike, my college roommate who had made the trek from Portland out to Montana for his first ever hunt. I had hung a stand for him just off a little round meadow where I had seen a great tall five by five skirting the night before. It wasn't hung too high, just 12 feet or so off of the ground. I showed Mike how to clip his harness onto the tether and he hoisted his bow up for some practice shots. He sat on the seat, quite still and gingerly pulled the bow back and fired his Judo point into a clump of brush. Good.

"Now go ahead and try one standing up."

Mike slowly and carefully stood up. His legs were fighting against his foolish brain that was telling him to stand. I could almost sense the world spinning around inside his head. He managed to try a shot, but before I could turn around to say anything, he had already plopped back onto the relative safety of the seat cushion. Heights were not his friend. Two rookies; two different learning experiences; both requiring trust in the teacher.

My son had watched me tie the climbing harness around his legs and over his shoulders. He had watched his father's strong hands tie the water knot into webbing and clip his harness into an unbreakable strength; me. He had felt me surrounding him as his feeble hands climbed the tree. He didn't even ask if the stand would hold him. It was made of metal. Nothing breaks metal.

My friend had watched as I told him to clip a carabineer that may or may not be strong enough into a rope that may or may not be weather-rotted. He climbed onto a stand that I had bought off the internet, and the safety stickers were peeling off. Who knows where this stand has been or how many times it has failed.

Jesus knew rookies when he saw them. His disciples wanted to follow him, but they were slow to trust him. They loved him yet denied him. They asked who would be the greatest in the kingdom of heaven. And Jesus' answer? Not the religious zealots. Not the passionate followers. Not those who were martyred for their faith. Little children. "I tell you the truth, unless you change and become like little children, you will never enter the kingdom of heaven." (Matthew 18:3)

That day, standing under my friend as he wrestled his way into the tree stand, fighting every logical and normal question that flies into a person's mind, I got a glimpse of what Jesus was saying. We can never be fully His until we fully trust his wisdom and power to protect us from the dangers of this world.

As Carson swung his feet out over the tree stand dangling from an aspen branch 15 feet in the air, he was fully surrendered. Dad said it would be alright, so it's alright. Dad tied the knots in my harness so they are tied perfectly and tight. Dad said he would never let me fall. I believe him. Period. At that point Carson was fully alive, fully passionate, and fully mine. Are you fully His?

Are you fully alive because you know that "to live is Christ and to die is gain"? (Philippians 1:21) Are you fully passionate because you recognize the magnitude of the cross and the sacrifice given on your behalf so that Christ could spend eternity with you without the chasm of sin between? Are you fully His? When Christ looks up the tree at the rookie in the stand, does he see your knees quaking or the soles of your shoes flying in the air because nothing can separate you from the love the Father has lavished on you?

"For I am convinced that neither death nor life, neither angels nor demons, neither the present nor the future, nor any powers, neither height nor depth, nor anything else in all creation, will be able to separate us from the love of God that is in Christ Jesus our Lord."
Romans 8:38-39

6. The Trail Camera

It was not the photo that I had expected to find on my trail camera. The camera had been set up at a creek crossing to see what animals had been using it. I also sweetened the area by spreading some peanut butter-honey mixture that I had left over from trapping season. As I scanned the photos on my computer, the one that surprised me was of my one and a half year old son eating the old bait off of the log using a stick as a utensil. You can see my butt off to the side as I was putting everything back in the pack. There, in those glowing pixels, was the proof of what had gone on. The only other proof that I got from the site was a couple of portraits of squirrels and countless photos of nothing, as the squirrels, birds or wandering toddlers had passed by too quickly to be captured.

I have learned some about using trail cameras over the past couple of years. I have hundreds of photos of waving grass. I no longer set my camera in areas of long grass. I have pictures of intense sun. Now I only face my camera north. I have pictures of deer butts and slow moving cattle. Now I aim my camera up the trail, not across it. There is one photo that has always captured my imagination. It was along a trail leading to the river. I had other photos of fawns and cattle as they meandered down for a drink. But this particular photo only shows the willows on the far side of the trail and small, light brown smudge on the left edge. Every time I look at that picture I try to make the crescent-shaped object into a deer tail, or a bird wing, or a hat hanging off a fisherman's pack. I will never know. If my camera had a faster trigger, the questions would be erased.

I want to leave no questions when asked about my faith. Now, you should know that my natural tendency is not outreach and seeking out converts. But I must know "the reason for the hope" that I profess. (I Peter 3:15) I can't give myself the option of having a slow trigger. When the Lord puts an opportunity for ministry right into my lap, I can't wait for a better time. If I'm to believe the gospel, the good news of Christ's redemption, then I must choose to embody it daily. I receive God's grace daily and therefore I must be ready to share the amazing story of that grace. "Preach the Word, be prepared in season and out of season, correct, rebuke, and encourage with great patience and careful instruction." (II Timothy 4:2) This was the charge to Timothy, a young pastor. Nowhere in that passage do we get the hint of "preach, when it fits your schedule, or when you are having a good day, or when you just studied your favorite scripture." We must be ready to pull the trigger now.

One of the biggest excuses that gets in the way of my testimony is my life itself. I stubbornly tell myself that the way I live my life will be a witness to that person that God has placed in front of me. And I hope that it is true of my life, but I don't think living the worthy life is the end-all to pulling the trigger. We must know, and be able to verbalize, the incredible gift of Christ's blood and the effect that it has on my life today as well as for eternity. When that is my mindset, I will always have a fast trigger. No matter the season.

"For what they were not told, they will see, and what they have not heard, they will understand."
Isaiah 52:15b

7. The Meat Pack

There is a picture that I love to hate. It is a fine picture of me weighted down with my new hunting pack. The back of the pack zips off so the frame can be used to haul meat. The meat bag is full and there is a symmetrical, bone-white four by four whitetail rack lashed to the outside. My gear bag is hanging in front of my chest. The image makes me look a little like the Beverly Hillbillies going camping. I love that part of the picture. The part that I hate is the miles of wind-swept plains that give way to snowcapped mountains way off in the distance and my truck is parked in those mountains.

Crossing three or so miles of rolling prairie I followed an oozing stream and was able to keep up a decent pace. My dad and other hunting partner didn't look too impatient as they cruised next to me. However, when we reached the foot of the mountain my partners took off after some deer they spotted in the bluffs off to our left. I began to question myself as the terrain turned vertical and each step stressed my body. Rest breaks came in clusters. My lungs struggled to keep up and my strength drained into the dry grass and rocks that I had to climb over. After a few hundred torturous vertical feet, I crested a bluff, and there sitting and chatting in front of me were my partners. I was drenched in sweat and gasping for breath while they were chatting about nothing in particular, just having a grand time. I collapsed next to them, a pile of beat up meat soaked in lactic acid.

To his credit, my partner John did offer to carry my pack for a while. But no, I shot the deer and I will finish this thing. And I did. We side-hilled up to the saddle and crossed over to the drainage with the truck. Flopping the meat pack into the bed of the truck, I had reached my goal. I had stuck it out for the long haul. I had made it!

Christ is interested in the long haul. No matter what your religious convictions; one cannot disregard a man that said he would do something and did it. Even if that task was giving your life in brutal crucifixion. Philippians tells us that Christ set aside his God-head and accepted the role of man in order to become the atoning sacrifice for a human race that despised him. And then He asks us to consider making Jesus' attitude our own. (Philippians 2:5)

Jesus really sets the cost of discipleship high in Luke 14:26. "If anyone comes to me and does not hate his father and mother, his wife and children, his brothers and sisters – yes even his own life – he cannot be my disciple. And anyone who does not carry his cross and follow me, cannot be my disciple." Now I don't think that Christ wants us to hate our families, as that is not consistent with the body of scripture. However, he makes it very clear that there is a type of passion and whole-person devotedness necessary to following Christ. If you do not count the steps leading you down the mountain, across the plains, and out to your deer, you may not be willing to carry it back. But if we will put to death our selfish pride and follow Christ, he will help us carry the load. Christ wants you to follow and he is also looking for people who are ready to die to themselves and stick it out for the long haul. Put on your meat pack and push hard for the mountains. He will be there waiting.

"And being found in appearance as a man, he humbled himself to death – even death on a cross. Therefore God exalted him to the highest place and gave him the name that is above every name. . . "
Philippians 2:8-9

8. The Grunt

I wanted more than anything to hear the awkward grunt call emanate from my hunting partner. We had chosen to set our stands about 80 yards from each other and I was seeing exactly what I hoped. Two does were filing out from the swamp and making their way down the trail, 30 yards in front of him. If I ducked down I could see his feet through the branches. He was standing, probably at full draw.

"Come on, grunt at them," I thought and wished. "Please, Mike, stop them."

But the deer calmly slipped past his stand. No shots were taken. The deer had no idea he was so close. The first deer on his first deer hunt had just passed my rookie friend.

The deer then made the fatal mistake and chose to walk to my stand. They passed the bush that was the 30-yard mark, but they were quartering too hard at me. They stepped over the 20-yard log with that clumsy deer walk that you only see from a stand. I didn't even know the range when they stepped from behind the tree at point blank distance. A little grunt from the back of my throat froze them in their tracks. I touched off an arrow and watched as my doe spun in disbelief, crashed through the quaking aspens painting them red and fell within sight. Perfect kill.

Mike was pleased that I had got my doe, but I could tell that his mind was still replaying the scene from a few minutes earlier. I could read it on his face, "If only I had grunted at them." I asked him about it later as I was packing out my meat. "Why didn't you stop them?"
"I panicked. I couldn't remember everything. I was thinking about being quiet and reaching my anchor and where to shoot and. . . . I forgot."

This was his first hunt though he had followed me around in the rain shadow of Mt. Hood in Oregon looking for deer. We saw seven deer all season. Now, for the first time, he had a bow in his hand and the ante was raised. His passion and excitement were personal now. So was his disappointment.

"If only I had called to them."

I must admit, that when I first started bow hunting, I had no idea how to stop a deer. I always just hoped it would work out. Much like Mike, I figured if I analyzed, checked and rechecked my abilities, and measured; I could do it on my own. I wonder how many opportunities for hunting glory literally walked right past me.

It wasn't until I sat in a sweltering hut in Nepal and listened to the firm voice of a Nepali missionary tell me that Christians want commitment, but Christ wants surrender, that I began to fully understand the heart of God. I will never forget those words. He wants his name to be on my every breath. He wants to be the most natural solution to me. He wants to hear my voice. He wants to hear me break myself before him. And in that brokenness, I will more clearly hear the voice of the Lord. I will not miss opportunities to conquer fear, to strengthen faith, to lift a burden, to meet a need, to enrich a life. In my surrender, I can hear the voice of God encouraging me to not let this opportunity simply walk by, even though it was in my range.

Stop measuring and analyzing. Start breathing surrender to Christ. Make it the most natural thing to you. When passions are at their peak, your adrenaline is high, your head spinning, and the opportunity to succeed or fail is right at your fingertips. You will not let that chance walk right out of range.

"Be wise in the way you act toward outsiders; make the most of every opportunity."
Colossians 4:5

9. The World's First GPS

As my dad and I searched for late season elk, something unusual happened. I looked at my dad and he looked at me and we totally disagreed as to where the truck was. We were standing on a lodgepole-choked ridge in a swirling snowstorm, and he was sure that we were supposed to drop down one side of the ridge, and I was sure it was the opposite way. The consequences of choosing the wrong side could be severe. There was a single road on one side and the other side dove off into a deep valley in the Frank Church River of No Return Wilderness area. It was almost dark and I looked at my dad, the man who had led me around the woods since I was literally an infant and said, "Let's go your way."

He was right. As we descended from the dizzying lodgepole out onto the broken slopes, the terrain started to look familiar. We dropped down to the truck exhausted, but pleased to have made it out. And we did it without a GPS.

My sons will grow up in a world knowing exactly where on this world they stand. When a GPS was simply a figment of my imagination, we were forced to use a map and compass and our own outdoor skills. My father drilled into me how to read and interpret the land and to be able to apply it to a map. Those were great skills to have, but I tended to be a little conservative when it came to launching off-trail across some unknown territory, especially into the wilderness where no roads can penetrate.

Now, with a few button-pushes on my $100 GPS, I can mark my truck and take off headlong into uncharted woods. I will be able to find my way back. My GPS knows the way. The biggest challenge that I now face is trying to remember what I named my truck using those few characters that my GPS will accept. Am I going to "TRK" or was it "TRCK"? It could be "TRK1" or two, or three. But aside from having to remember a few little letters, my mind tells me that you can go wherever you want. Trust the GPS.

The Israelites were experienced in GPS use. Not that they had electronics while they were wandering in the desert, but rather, they followed a pillar of cloud and of fire; the first GPS. They had been enslaved in Egypt for 430 years. Now, after the slave generations had passed they took off headlong into desert. But they didn't need to fear, they could see, plain as day, the path that God had chosen for them. "Just keep following the cloud." It's almost like following that little arrow on my GPS. It shows me the way back to Canaan. (Or was is "CANN" or "CNAN"?)

The challenging part of this Christian walk is being able to trust our GPS. Do we have such a relationship with the Lord that we can clearly see Him leading us? One of my favorite verses in the Bible is Isaiah 30:21, "Whether you turn to the right or to the left, your ears will hear a voice behind you, saying, "This is the way; walk in it." Notice that it does not say God will always give us a blazing fireball or a cloud to direct our path. He promises a voice behind you. If we are to recognize that still small voice of the Holy Spirit, we must be familiar with the nature of God. In order for there to be trust, there must be relationship.

When I looked at my dad's face on top of that windswept ridge, I saw the same red beard that covered my dad's confidant smile since I was an infant. I saw the same look in his eyes, that he will never do anything to hurt me. I saw a man who had invested so much into me. That voice I can trust. I know him. Do you know the voice of the Father? Would he sound foreign on the other end of a phone call? Your answer to that question will dictate your ability to respond to the all-powerful God of the universe. You will be prepared to step off the ridge with the cloud in front of you and the voice behind and it is leading straight to "HEAVN".

"By day, the Lord went ahead of them in a pillar of cloud to guide them on their way and by night in a pillar of fire, so that they could travel by day or night."

Exodus 13:21

10. The Wrong End of the Binoculars

My two-year-old son sat bouncing along in his car seat jammed between my hunting partner, John, and I as we headed up to some mule deer breaks. Usually a pretty quiet kid around other people, Carson broke the silence and asked for my partner's binoculars. I tried to save him the greasy fingerprints that I knew were inevitable by offering my binoculars as a substitute. But no, Carson had his heart set on my buddy's brand new glass. John handed over the binoculars and watched as the wobbly hands of my kid immediately draped the strap around his neck and brought the binoculars to his little eyes; backwards.

We both kind of laughed and showed him how to turn them the right way, but in his toddling insolence, Carson demanded that he look through them backwards. I wondered how far the dashboard must look peering the wrong way through binoculars. Those knobs and dials that were only a couple of feet in front of him appeared to be far away, down a distant tunnel. Carson didn't get the point of binoculars; to bring the distant up close.

I love hunting elk in the south end of the Bitterroot valley in Montana. I don't hunt deer there, because the tag is next to impossible to draw, but on a September afternoon, it was mule deer that I was glassing. I had seen a nice four by four get up out of his bed and sat down to watch. It was only when I lifted my binoculars that I noticed he wasn't alone. In fact just off to his left, lay the biggest typical buck I have ever laid eyes on. His deep back forks towered over his head and then forked again. He sat there peering around with a magnificent six by six rack. I sat slack jawed wishing that my number had been drawn for that tag, when a giant nontypical appeared from behind some brush. Although not heavy, his rack must have sported 20 points on a side; junk points were everywhere. I was witnessing pure beauty. And it was beauty I never would have seen had I not taken the time to use my binoculars.

My binoculars didn't change that bachelor group of mule deer, but they did change my perspective of the deer. All too often in our Christian walk, we use our binoculars the wrong way. We are attempting to look at God, to better understand him, but we have a borrowed pair of binoculars stubbornly focusing the wrong way. God appears distant and blurry. His grace, hope and love seem to be down a hall of mirrors that we can never travel. But yet we sit in church and frequently sing songs of which the theme is to magnify the Lord. Think about that. Magnify the Lord. Nothing in that phrase calls for God, the omnipotent, omniscient, omnipresent Creator of the universe to change. On the contrary, when we magnify the Lord, we are simply changing our perspective of him. "Jesus Christ is the same yesterday and today and forever." (Hebrews 13:8) He is the unchangeable God who sits on his thrown extending all goodness and grace to us. Be careful not to get greasy fingerprints on your perspective. If God seems distant, flip your perspective around and allow his Spirit to clarify his being and all the nontypical gifts he has for you.

A couple of days later as we sat around watching Carson open his birthday presents, he unwrapped a small rectangular gift; binoculars. Complements of John.

"[A]nd let us draw near to God with a sincere heart in full assurance of faith, having our hearts sprinkled to cleanse us from a guilty conscience and having our bodies washed with pure water."
Hebrews 10:22

11. Cut on Contact

"This is going to be easy!" I thought as I followed my first faux blood trail my archery hunter safety instructor had made. I hardly had to connect the dots. It was more like following the solid string of "blood" he laid down through the bushes behind our classroom. It looked like he had poked a hole in the bottom of a can of red paint and gone for a stroll. I could have swore at that teacher a few years later as I was waist deep in a swampy pond, swinging my flashlight around looking for any blood on cattails or a patch of disturbed mud that might be evidence that the little buck I had arrowed two hours earlier had passed by. This was not a walk in the park.

While my instructor's blood trail example had left much to be desired, I do remember his broadhead lesson. He took a piece of elk skin leather and pushed different kinds of broadheads through it in order to show the relative amounts of energy each type took. A dull replaceable blade broadhead took some muscling to push through. A sharp one still took some effort, but was a lot easier. And then he brought out a cut-on-contact head. He simply laid the skin over the top of the vertical arrow and with just a little wiggling the broadhead went right through the hide. The weight of the hide itself was enough to split it wide open.

And split wide open is the goal. The less energy our broadhead uses getting inside the quarry, the better chance the arrow has of blowing out the other side and completing the job in between. That is the singular responsibility of a broadhead. Its job is to cut.

We have specific jobs as part of the family of God as well. One of those jobs is to correct a brother when he falls into sin. Luke 17:3b sums it up, "If your brother sins, rebuke him, and if he repents, forgive him." That seems very straight forward and to the point. If your brother sins, rebuke him. That is what I call "cut-on-contact" discipleship. There is no wasted energy in opening up a mechanical blade or pushing a round metal point through the "hide". Rather, when he sins rebuke him. Cut on contact. Don't waste time pampering. Of course with our cut-on-contact mindset, we must be careful that we are rebuking our brothers in Christ, who know and understand the will of God. It is the secular world looking in at the church that may describe us as judgmental. And we are called to judge. In a world that is being spun away by humanistic worldviews and an "anything goes" attitude, we are called to listen to the Spirit and call sin what it is. And here is where the chasm forms between the church and skeptics. Scripture calls us to love the sinner and scripture calls us to hate sin. The distinction between those two phrases will enable us to be effective in Christ's community. We also must realize that the ultimate cut-on-contact moment will occur for all of us at judgment.

But in the mean time, call "sin" sin and be ready to watch your brother's life improve.

"He who rebukes a man will in the end gain more favor than he who has a flattering tongue."

Proverbs 28:23

12. The Glow Stick

I was following hand signals through the December-deep snow circling above an elk that we had watched bed down. As the cow stood from her bed, one shot from my .54 caliber muzzleloader is all that it took to pile her up at the base of a massive Douglas fir. Being right at dusk, my father and I met at the elk for a short celebration. We were two hours away from the truck; it was going to be a long night. I pulled out my headlamp in order to start field dressing my prize. But as I went to turn it on, I found the switch already on and the batteries dead. I worked as fast as I could in the waning light, but soon it was just too dark. I rummaged through my pack with my bloody-yet-freezing hands and found a glow stick. Qualifying the scenario as a "light" emergency, I snapped the stick and went back to work in the alien green glow.

It wasn't gutting the elk by glow stick that remains such a vivid memory to me. It was the meat-laden hike out. With no flashlights, we headed down the familiar valley. Coming around a corner, we were met by the rising moon. The snowy landscape glowed and silhouetted the pines black. We could see each post-holed step we had taken on our ascent. Though my legs burned and I wanted nothing more than to be back at the truck, the scene struck me as being perfect. There I was sweating in two feet of snow while the temperature was single digits. I was walking at night, but it wasn't really dark at all. In fact, the light afforded by the moon illuminated everything that I truly cared about; the path home.

I laugh now at the image of me diving into an elk's chest cavity armed with a knife and a glow stick. The glow stick speckled with blood was barely enough light to see beyond the tip of my nose but it did get the job done. I wonder too, how often I am perfectly content trusting the light of my own judgment which is about as bright as that glow stick, when my Savior is available as the divine light for my life. He said, "I am the light of the world. Whoever follows me will never walk in darkness, but will have the light of life." (John 8:12) Just like the moonlight that night, the wisdom of God surrounds us and takes us to places that we don't even know. You and I are capable of a mere glow stick's worth of knowledge and foresight. But the Lord's understanding spreads infinitely like the sense I felt when I stepped into the moonlight that night. It was when I stopped relying on the pale imitation of light that I found the Lord illuminating the path home.

"If I say, 'Surely the darkness will hide me and the light become night around me,; even the darkness will not be dark to you; the night will shine like day for the darkness is as light to you."
Psalm 139 11-12

13. The Garbage Bag Canteen

In the tiny zipper pouch on the bottom of my hunting pack is a black garbage bag. I keep it tucked down there for a variety of purposes, but my favorite is to store backstraps after I quarter an animal up on the ridge.

On opening day of archery season I found myself drudging up the mountain to a waterhole some 1,000 vertical feet above me. The penetrating darkness seemed to swallow me up as I rarely use a flashlight when hiking in the dark. Every once in a while I would pause and take a tiny sip of water out of my hydration pack. I didn't want to tank up before a long sit in the treestand. I could hear a bull bugling up beyond the stand and my heart was pounding with exhaustion and anticipation. I climbed up into my stand under the now-gray sky and waited. The bull didn't visit me that morning though I could hear him shuffling his cows around just out of sight.

I watched until noon and decided to stretch my legs. I lowered my pack and bow out of the stand with my trusty parachute cord. About half way to the ground the rope snapped and sent my gear tumbling down. I hustled to the ground and found the most substantial damage to be the removal of the bite tip used for my hydration pack. After repairing it, I checked my water level. What had been over two liters of water was now only a trickle in the hose. It had all leaked out! Disappointed, but not worried, I went on with a midday hunt and returned to sit in the stand for the evening.

The sip of water in the hose had been used up and now I was starting to feel the effects of all that climbing without water. The dark clouds that had been banking up all afternoon were now consuming the mountainside and it wasn't long before a torrential downpour hit. I tipped my head back to capture some drops like a child catching snowflakes, but my thirst wasn't quenched. Finally, after huddling against the trunk of the tree, my mind flashed to the garbage bag in the bottom of my pack.

I pulled out the bag, laid it over my legs and formed a little well in the middle. In only a few minutes it was filling nicely and I bent over and sucked down nice cold drinks. I had never been more pleased than to be drinking out of a garbage bag!

I suppose that drinking from a garbage bag might be unthinkable by some. Scripture teaches us how to deal with suffering; by adding joy. While those two words are essentially antonyms, Paul connects the dots for us. "Not only so, but we also rejoice in our sufferings, because we know that suffering produces perseverance; perseverance, character; and character, hope." (Romans 5:3) In thinking back to that soggy day in the stand, I too can see how drinking out of a garbage bag allowed me to stay on stand. Even when the mocking text messages began to come in

41

from my wife who was warm and dry indoors, I kept standing. The water that I received from the bag powered the rest of the day. As I looked at that black garbage bag, my mind began to shift once more, from thirst to the real reason for the bag; backstraps. From despair to hope. And that is precisely what the Lord wants us to see as we face our sufferings. Sitting in our soaking wet, cold, dehydrated laps is a thin, black plastic bag of hope.

"Perseverance must finish its work in you so that you may be mature and complete, not lacking anything."
James 1:4

14. The Range Finder

I knew it was about 35 yards. Maybe 40. Or just a touch over 40. The distance was hard to judge as my wife and I sat huddled behind an overgrown sage watching the edge of a dying waterhole. Depending on where the deer came in, they would be just at the edge of my shooting range. As it so happened on that frigid September afternoon, the band of three does popped up over the lip beyond the pond and worked their way to the right side before deciding to take a drink. By my estimation the lead doe was about 43 yards away when I drew my bow. I changed my mind on the estimation of distance a split second later as my arrow zipped over her back, splashing into the mud beyond. Too high. This being the first time my wife had accompanied me bow hunting, I was sure that she was beginning to doubt my skills. I trudged the distance to retrieve my muddy arrow. 33…34…35. 35 yards to the set of tracks that the doe had left on her quick departure. I had misjudged the distance and I had a doe tag in my pocket to prove it.

I figured that my luck had run out and I settled in behind the sage again. Jolene made sure to keep her eyes on her magazine so as not to give me the look that I knew she wanted too. I sat there, pulling my collar up against the cold wind and waited. But my luck had not run out. As the magical hour approached I saw a nice four by four whitetail approach from the opposite side of the pond. My adrenaline exploded and a million doubts ran through my head. What if I misjudge again? I could know for sure if he went to the pond at the same place as the doe. I couldn't wish for that. But in fact, the buck stooped his head right above tracks left by the doe a few minutes earlier. I split the 30 and 40 yard pins on his chest and touched off the arrow. Ted Nugent calls it the "mystical flight" of the arrow. And in that case, I must say I admired the flight of that arrow as it pounded into the chest of my first bow-kill. The buck left an easy blood trail and it didn't take long until I was standing over the beautiful buck with my now-proud bride beside me. All I had to know was the distance.

The imperfect steps that I used to pace off the distance to the pond have been replaced by a laser range finder that fits in the palm of my hand. Click on the pond, it reads 35. Click on that little clump of knapweed off to the side, 47. Click on the fencepost to my left, 18. Click. Click. Click. It is all laid out with the clarity of little digital number in the corner of the screen. Now I really know the distance, and I have confidence in my shot.

Christ knew the distance too. He knew how many agonizing steps to the top of Golgotha. He knew the price He would pay for our sins. And yet He put one shaky, blood-drenched foot in front of the other all the way to the top of that hill. He knew the distance and still walked it. He knew how long He would be in the grave before He would overcome the curse of death.

We are to count the cost, not after we have buried an arrow into the mud; but before. There will be a cost to following Christ. We are not promised an easy stroll to Paradise. Rather we are told that we will be tested, bent and bruised. Though the road may be rocky and dangerous, God offers us hope in James 1:2-4. "Consider it pure joy, my brothers, whenever you face trials of many kinds, because you know that the testing of your faith develops perseverance. Perseverance must finish its work so that you may be mature and complete, not lacking anything." There is reward at the end of the road. But we cannot come up short. If we choose to make the journey without first measuring the distance, we will come up short. Our human nature will take us down the path of least resistance which ultimately leads to destruction. We must be ready. We must count the cost. We must measure the distance. And once measured, we move with confidence toward our goal. And that mystical flight leads straight to Paradise.

"'Love the Lord your God with all your heart and with all your soul and with all your strength and with all your mind. . .'"
Luke 10:27

15. The Nock

My 8-year-old eyes were the size of saucers as I watched the hunting circus unfold before my eyes. Being too young to have experienced buck fever myself, I had a front row seat to watching a grown man turn into an incompetent, fumbling idiot. You see, my family was returning home after spending the afternoon with friends that lived a short distance out of town. As we were driving the sluggish brown station wagon home, a nice mule deer buck sauntered across the road in front of us. Not having his bow along, my dad flipped a U-turn and headed back to get our friend Don who had never arrowed an animal. After racing around the garage to grab his quiver and bow, Don came bounding out to our car and we were racing back to the place we had seen the buck.

The next portion of time probably only lasted a few seconds, but in my mind it was a comical eternity. Don climbed the embankment where the deer had last been seen, and as mule deer often do, the buck had only moved off a few yards. I couldn't see the deer from my seat in the station wagon, but I could tell by his frantic body language that Don could see him. Don fumbled with an arrow, hurriedly nocked it, and pulled back so quickly that the arrow fell off the rest. He attempted to jiggle the arrow back onto the rest without letting down. Having failed at this, he let down, and got the arrow back on the shelf, all the while glancing nervously in the direction of the buck.

This time Don ran his finger on the arrow as he drew and promptly pulled it off the string as he horsed it back. Again, he let down, nocked the arrow, came to full draw and amazingly released the shot. I could hear the loud crack of the impact and quickly Don hunched over to see where the buck had run through the thick trees. A couple of seconds later, a three by three muley with an arrow dangling from its shoulder popped across the road and barreled down through the dark timber toward the river.

We all got out and picked up the blood trail in the fading light which led straight down the mountain through the pines and ended at the river. Dejected, we discussed the possibility of the deer successfully swimming the river in his condition. Someone noticed that downstream and on the far side of the river in a neatly manicured lawn, up by the porch, lay the dead buck.

Equally unexpected, the elderly woman who lived there opened the door before we could even knock and simply asked if we would like the porch light on to help with tending to the deer.

I suppose that the most remarkable part of this hunt was that it was successful at all. Imagine, in the hubbub, watching Don attempt to nock his arrow at precisely the right location to maximize arrow flight. It would be impossible without the aid of the nock. The nock was placed on the string in the controlled environment of the pro-shop. The string was measured and squared and the nock placed at exactly the right position. Exactly where the arrow belongs.

I find it interesting that often in the Old Testament the Israelites would leave a marker, a reminder, of when they were exactly where they belonged. When Jacob had his dream about angels coming and going from heaven, he left a pillar of rock, a nock, calling it "House of God". It was at that place that God spoke to Jacob and made his future covenant clear. God would be with Jacob and his offspring. That is something that must be remembered.

When the Israelites banded together under Joshua and promised to follow God, they left a nock. And prior to that, when Joshua led the Israelites into the land promised to them, God instructed them to erect a nock. Remember what it was like to follow God. It was a controlled measured experience, one that needed to be remembered. And not just remembered at that moment, but that experience needed to be remembered by future generations as well. God told Joshua that when your children return and ask about the twelve stones, he could tell them of the miracle. In other words, life will get chaotic, we will wander, but if we remember the nock and its purpose, we know exactly where to return.

Needless to say, I was deeply pleased when I found my 3-year-old teaching his little buddy how to shoot a longbow. Hold it this way, and grab the arrow here, and put the orange feather out, and the arrow snaps on right here. At the nock.

"'Be strong, all you people of the land,' declares the Lord, 'and work. For I am with you,' declares the Lord Almighty. 'This is what I covenanted with you when you came out of Egypt. And my spirit remains among you. Do not fear.'"

Haggai 2:4b-5

16. The Wind Checker

I could feel his bugle rattling in my chest. Every guttural scream the bull let out seemed to echo off the bare trunks of the burn that I was hunting. My hunting partner and I had heard this bull bugling as we snuck down the gated logging road in the inky darkness. It was too early to shoot, but we wanted to get close so that when the light was good, we would be within striking distance. We positioned ourselves below the bull and his harem and checked the wind. Perfect. The cool morning air was just barely sliding down the ridge right into our faces. We slowly eased up through the burn, letting out soft cow calls. With every "mew" the bull screamed back before we could even finish calling. We were close.

We could hear the massive bull thrashing away at a dead blowdown. His antlers were scraping and rattling against the wood with incredible force. My partner motioned for me to move up ahead and be the shooter while he stayed behind to call the bull past my position. I set up at the base of a large tree and checked the wind.

Almost dead calm. The sun was now hitting the trees on the top of the ridge where the bull was keeping tabs on his harem; a mere 80 yards away.

The cows and spikes started filtering across the ridge in front of me. I knew it was only a matter of minutes or even seconds before the herd bull showed himself. All of a sudden the bull stopped raking his antlers and the cows' heads popped up from their feeding. In a few precious seconds, the woods were filled with alarm barks as the herd bull gathered up his harem and disappeared over the ridge. I sat there dumbfounded, seeing the image of the big bull, his long main beams arching over his back, looping across the ridge, pushing the cows over the top. How did that happen? That is when I reached into my pocket, found my wind checker and watched as the cursed little puff of white powder drifted effortlessly up the ridge. Winded.

It doesn't take much to shift the wind. The rays of the sun warming up that burned hillside cost me a chance at a great bull by switching the air currents. It doesn't take much to shift a good Christian life away from the currents of the Lord's will. As believers, it is of the utmost importance that we constantly check the wind. No, we don't have a little bottle of spiritual powder that we can puff into the air, but we do have the still, small voice of the Holy Spirit that breathes into our lives when we are attentive. It is easy to watch my hunting wind checker send little clouds into the air. It is not, however, as easy to be alert to the working of the Holy Spirit. It takes time with the Lord. And it takes an uninsulated heart to hear that voice.

I remember hunting late season elk with my dad in my early teens. We had just spent a long morning trudging through snow searching for any sign of elk. We always hiked ourselves to exhaustion. It was great. We were returning to our vehicle when a nice new truck plowed up next to us. As he rolled down his window, cigarette smoke and rock and roll poured out. There he was, sitting in his T-shirt with his loaded gun on the seat right next to him. In that truck was the best example of an insulated hunter I have ever seen.

"Seen anything?" he asked. We just had to smile.

Short of a tornado, he wouldn't have been able to tell which way the wind was blowing, or even cared for that matter. "Do not be misled: 'Bad company corrupts good character.' Come back to your senses as you ought, and stop sinning; for there are some who are ignorant of God – I say this to your shame." (I Corinthians 15:33-34) This verse speaks about the insulated hunter, calling him ignorant of God. How easily we let the influences of the world ruin our chances to enjoy the blessings of God. Listen to the Holy Spirit; that still small voice urging you into the currents of the Lord so that you will not become shameful and ignorant. Check the wind frequently and you will find yourself at full draw in that perfect set-up that God has destined you for.

"Show me your ways, O Lord, teach me your paths; guide me in your truth and teach me, for you are God my Savior, and my hope is in you all day long."
Psalm 25:4-5

17. The Spine

All I could think of was the twelve dozen golden aluminum arrows sitting in my garage, wasted. I had taken my newly purchased bow to a pro-shop to see why the broadheads shot so poorly. As I set my bow and arrow on the counter, the guy behind the glass counter took one look at my arrows and said, "You're missing down and to the right, aren't you?" Exactly.

"You're lucky that you haven't blown one of these arrows up on your rest. These are spined for 35 pounds and you are shooting 65!"

Money was tight for me as a junior in high school, and I began to mourn the fact that all those brand new arrows I had bought with my bow were just taking up space, useless. The spine was too weak; they couldn't stand up under the pressure.

When our faith is under-spined, we run the risk of breaking and we definitely won't hit the mark. It is clear from the book of Job that God allows us to be tested; spined. The testing of our faith can come from all angles, but Satan's goal is singular; make us turn away from God. God has a perfect plan and hope for your life, but in order to hit the target, we must be shot like arrows. I have learned that as the bow shoots, the arrow must bend and flex as the energy is transferred. Faith is the spine that gives us stability and courage when we are tested. God also knows just how much pressure we can take before we fold into a pile of worthless gold-colored aluminum. I Corinthians 10:13 says, "No temptation has seized you except what is common to man. And God is faithful; he will not let you be tempted beyond what you can bear." God has designed you for a purpose. And to accomplish that purpose you must be able to stand up under it.

Imagine the responsibility that Jesus had. Live a perfect life, stand up to a lifetime of temptation, and then become the blameless sacrifice enduring unimaginable pain. And what did God do to test His spine? He sent Jesus to the desert for 40 days of one on one with Satan. Do you remember what Christ used to battle the devil in that tempting time? The Word of God. His faith was based on the truth of God's word. He believed it and trusted it. Jesus quoted from the Old Testament to fend off the pressures of the supreme tempter. Sounds like a good model to me. Build your own spine by saturating yourself in the Word. I don't want to have the spine of my golden arrows, which are now being used by the neighbor kids and drug around the yard as swords for my toddlers. I want to be strong, ready to be used as a lethal weapon in God's quiver.

"And the God of all grace who called you to his eternal glory in Christ, after you have suffered a little while, will himself restore you and make you strong, firm and steadfast."
I Peter 5:10

18. The Hydration Pack

The short end of the stick never felt as short as when I turned my collar and face mask to a sharp wind at 30 degrees below zero. My partner and I were bowhunting elk at the end of a frigid Montana December. We had found the fence crossing where the elk left the ranch and the idea was that one of us would hunker down in the trees next to the crossing while the other drove a couple of miles away and pushed the herd across the prairie and up into the protection of the trees.

With the wind tearing at my face, I closed my eyes, lowered my shoulder and pushed across the flat. It took only seconds to find the chinks in my armor as I fidgeted with my balaclava, hat, gloves and coat trying my best to battle the elements.

I climbed up a steep sagebrush bluff and found a cluster of trees to take a break. Reaching back for my hydration tube, I heard a cracking as it had frozen solid. I slid off my pack and rummaged around for the hydration bladder. It hadn't frozen yet, so I quickly got my drink and shoved it back into the relative warmth of my day pack.

I covered the two miles up to my partner and can say confidently that if the band of cows that I had pushed to him had actually crossed within bow range, he never would have been able to draw his bow. He sat their huddled and shivering on a little patch of dry ground under a huge Douglas fir. His arms, legs and equipment were all frozen too. We looked at each other with that "What the heck are we doing" look and turned back toward the truck for shelter against the unbearably cold environment.

The Israelites at the time of Jeremiah had a harsh environment too, though it was one of their own making. The book of Jeremiah is filled with warnings for being distant from God through sin. He implores the lost to come back to Himself. The closer His beloved children were to His heart, the more His blessings could flow into their lives.

The Lord describes his passion for His people in Jeremiah 31:3. "I have loved you with an everlasting love; I have drawn you with loving kindness." In the next three verses he describes what life will be like in His presence. The obvious inference is that out of His presence, the environment is pretty bleak. There would be destruction, no singing, no dancing, crops would fail to produce. Life would be hopeless, without joy. So just like the line in my hydration pack, the further from the center, the colder it gets.

When our fellowship with God is broken and love fails to flow, we get a sense of lack of joy when apart from God. In verses four, five and six of chapter 31, we see that after being drawn to the center close to God's loving heart, the builders will build, the farmers will plant and reap, the watchmen will cry out. Each of these vocations finds success in doing what they were designed to do when they are enveloped by God's loving-kindness. Unlike the water in the hose that froze solid and was rendered useless in a matter of minutes, so we who seek the Lord will be more effective when we are in the warm folds of God's embrace. In that place, there are no short straws.

"He is my loving God and my fortress, my stronghold and my deliverer, my shield, in whom I take refuge, who subdues peoples under me."
Psalm 144:2

19. The Cover Scent

There is a stretch of 76 miles of washboarded, uncomfortable dirt road that I love more than any other. It is the road that stretches between towering granite walls from my childhood town to the little cabin that we rented, for the price of repairs, to hunt elk. It was over those 76 miles that my dad and I would take our yearly pilgrimage to hunt the building herds of elk as they bottlenecked on their way to the Salmon River breaks. I remember gladly waking up at horrific hours of the morning to trek up the broken slopes searching for elk. It was on that slope that I shot my first elk. My uncle and I had climbed the snow-covered mountain in the inky darkness of pre-dawn. As we moved across the open hillsides with brushy avalanche chutes, we jumped a herd if feeding cows. Both of us shot our first elk and we watched as they slid headlong to the bottom. It is, and always will be, one of my fondest memories.

On that hillside is a plant called ceanothus. The stubborn, thick leaves hang on when all other deciduous plants have given up the battle. As I climbed those hills in the snow, I would strip off an occasional leaf in my gloved hand, crush it, and breath in the rich, musky, almost animal smell that said "elk country" to me.

Seventeen years after my first elk, I was driving with my wife down a dirt road, not in search of elk, but ceanothus. Clipping down the road, I spotted one lonely bush out of the corner of my eye. I slammed on the brakes, jammed the Honda in reverse, and backed up next to a perfect specimen. I hopped out of the car, armed with my Wal-Mart bag and joyfully went about collecting the leaves of elk country.

"Smells like pee," was the short remark my generally uninterested wife made after I encouraged her to breath deep the beautiful scent. I slumped down behind the steering wheel extremely disappointed. Here I have driven up into the high country with the express purpose of collecting ceanothus to make the most nostalgic cover scent and my wife thinks I will be spraying "pee" on myself. As serious hunters know, we all give off a scent. It was my hope to make my scent that of elk country; one of the most beautiful and invigorating scents. But to my wife I had collected leaves to make urine tea. Same smell, very different meaning.

"But thanks be to God, who always leads us in triumphal procession in Christ and through us spreads everywhere the fragrance of the knowledge of him. For we are to God the aroma of Christ among those who are being saved and those who are perishing. To one we are the smell of death; to the other, the fragrance of life. And who is equal to such a task." (II Corinthians 2:14-16)

Those of us who are in Christ are meant to be the aroma of God to everyone around us. Now that is a lot of pressure! I am to be that symbol to a person that causes their heart and soul to leap to that nostalgic place of comfort and peace. Or maybe it isn't nostalgic to someone who has never heard of the love of God. You are their first sniff!

As we go about our day, living out our walks, we will encounter those who are repulsed by the smell of God. Unresolved sin can build up in a person's life and when they are faced with a God who is wholly loving, but also entirely just, the aroma seems dangerous. And in fact it is! Without the mediation of Christ, we are trapped in sin and will always find God acrid. Share the love of Christ and let your aroma be that perfect stalk up the ridge to the Creator.

"Live such good lives among the pagans that, though they accuse you of doing wrong, they may see your good deeds and glorify God on the day he visits us."
I Peter 2:12

20. The Messy Pack

It seems odd that after hunting with my dad for 18 years that one of my fondest hunting memories would be of sharing a Pepsi and a Snickers. I would follow him up and down mountains in search of quarry, my short strides reaching to match his footsteps. I remember exerting myself, trying to keep up. And when my stubby little legs failed, my dad would pull up a log, and go digging in his daypack. We never drank our own cans of pop, we always shared. And if we were hunting after Halloween, there would be a tiny candy bar for each of us.

I can still remember the shot of energy that the sugar would send through my veins. I felt like a new man! It didn't matter where we were hunting, whether the high elevation forests, river bottoms, or the Salmon River breaks, my dad always new when it was time to break open the daypack. I still carry around cans of Pepsi, but I've found that the trick-or-treating success seriously slows after age 20. So now I am relegated to either buying candy, which I rarely do, or carrying a granola bar. And it was that granola bar that changed my backpack forever.

The end of the long season had come. I had chased elk with my bow in –20 ° F weather and, having come up empty, decided it was time to hang up my bow for the year. I briefly sorted through my pack and threw it up on the nail in my garage. Winter passed and as summer trudged on, it came time for me to start the premature fidgeting with my hunting gear. As I pulled my pack off the nail, I noticed a quarter-sized hole in the top. I pulled on the zippers and peered inside, my heart sank. The interior of my pack was full of mouse poop. I carefully dug to the bottom of the pack and found the problem. I had left an old granola bar in the depths of my pack, which the mouse had found and chewed. My pack and all the gear were coated in musky mouse waste. It took a long time of careful washing to get the gear back to working condition, and the pack itself never did return to action. A granola bar that I had hoped to enjoy while sitting on a log smelling the sweet essence of September had led to a mouse outhouse.

Like the granola bar in my pack, the gifts of the Holy Spirit can waste away if they slide to the bottom of our pack. God gave us the Holy Spirit as a power source, a Counselor and Encourager. His communion is something to be relished. Like a weary kid trudging after his father, we can often find ourselves slogging through life, gasping for breath. And like my father did, our heavenly Father knows just when to pull up a log and open up a gift that is beyond sugar. The comfort, guidance and encouragement that comes from having communion with the Holy God does so much more than pump our veins with a temporary sugar high. Our life is renewed by the presence of the Lord. And when we are strong and don't bury that gift deep in our life, the blessing is spread. So don't hang the pack of your life on a nail with God's gifts rotting in the bottom, rather pull them out and make a memory filled with the aroma of September, not of a mouse.

"If you then, though you are evil, know how to give good gifts to your children, how much more will your Father in heaven give the Holy Spirit to those who ask him!"
Luke 11:13

21. The Hoochie Mama

I was helping my brother-in-law move some old hunting equipment down into his basement when I noticed a piece of flexible plumbing pipe sticking out of a tattered box.

"Do you want this pipe in here?" I asked in all sincerity.

He looked at the "pipe" and laughed. It wasn't plumbing at all! As a matter of fact, it was the first elk bugle he had ever used. He uncoiled the flexible pipe and blew into one end. A high-pitched, nasal whine pierced my ears. The harder he blew; the tone would step up in a chunky scale.

"This used to really bring in the bulls."

I couldn't believe that any animal, especially wary, mature bulls would do anything but run away from the annoying sound. It was especially surprising since in my few years of calling elk, I had spent a ridiculous amount of money on gimmicks and kits, all in the name of calling elk in September. I remember sitting as a kid in front of a rented hunting video repeatedly playing and rewinding a calling sequence as I tried to emulate it using a bargain-bin turkey diaphragm.

I have bought calls in all shapes and sizes; single reed, double reed, estrous, diaphragms with slits and domes. All these added more and more complexity to the nature of calling elk. Then I discovered the little, gray push-button call titled the "Hoochie Mama." Overcoming my initial hesitation to buy a call with such risqué insinuations, I found the easiest way possible to call elk. Push the button. That is it. Push the button. As you depress the bellows, a gentle sliding cow call emanates, ending in that edgy chirp that only a cow elk can do. Now here is a call that I can use.

Undoubtedly in a couple of years, my sons will be following me into the yellowed tamaracks armed with Hoochie Mama calls, ready to call for dad. I don't have to explain to them how to fit a diaphragm call to the roof of their mouths. I don't have to show them the angle to blow across the reed, or how long to hold the note, or whether or not to slide at the end. Push the button.

It is simplicity that attracted me to the call. And it is that simplicity with which I want my sons to approach their faith in the Lord. While the Bible has hundreds of pages that all point to Christ and how to live in Him, what is it that I want to explain to my kids? I John 3:23 lays it out pretty clearly. "And this is his command: to believe in the name of his Son, Jesus Christ, and to love one another as he commanded us."

That is it. That is the button that I want my boys to push. Now don't get me wrong, I don't think that they should ignore the rest of the Bible because they understand that verse. On the contrary, as they grow and mature they will discover the many ways that God the Father has authored the scripture to work in unity as His voice.

When in the woods, I still carry a daypack pocket full of calls. I even hike with my favorite diaphragm in my cheek. But through the use of all these tools, I can be confidant that when my mouth goes dry, or I can't find the right tone of estrous call, I can still push the button. When we can't find the right verse, or hear His voice over the clamor of our lives, we can push the button. We can believe, like scripture says, and we can love. Christ will be with us to help us show his love to the world. Push the button.

"Love the Lord your God with all you heart and with all your soul and with all your mind and with all your strength. The second is this: 'Love your neighbor as yourself.' There is no commandment greater than these."
Mark 12:30-31

22. Slave to the Safety Harness

I have never been so mad at a little piece of webbing. It was because of the webbing tether that goes from my safety harness to the tree that I was now looking at the white end of a whitetail rather than celebrating a perfect hunt. The worst part, it was the second night in a row that it had happened.

My treestand set was perfect. It was 13 yards off of a major travel corridor in a small clump of ponderosas. My stand was in the back tree with two in front of me. The idea was that as the deer walked by, I would draw when their head went behind one of the front trees and then I would drop them with a great, short shot as they stepped out. The night before, two four by four bucks had come wandering down my trail. As the first one went behind my drawing tree, I pulled back my bow and bumped my elbow on the bark of the tree. That tiny little crunch was enough to freeze that buck in his tracks. He left without me being able to get a shot.

The next night I was back in the stand. The same two bucks came down the trail. I was not going to make that mistake twice. I stood up ever so slowly. I leaned out as far from the tree as possible. There was no way my elbow could hit the bark now. The first, bigger, buck went behind the drawing tree. I slowly pulled back my compound and to my horror, there was a little swoosh sound as my elbow slid past the now-tight safety tether. The horrific scene from the night before replayed exactly. The buck flipped a U-turn and flagged away to about 80 yards where he and his buddy stared, snorting, back at the tree that had scared them two nights in a row. Oh, if only I hadn't been wearing my harness! I would have had a nice buck that night.

In reality, if I did not have my harness on that night and actually put the arrow into the vitals of that deer, I would have probably gotten weak-kneed and taken a fall right out of that stand. Then my wife would be saying "Oh, if he had only been wearing his harness." You see there are choices to be made. While I am still bitter about losing that buck, I understand the effects of gravity. I prefer to be tied to a tree. And ultimately, that harness could save me from a deadly fall and actually extend my hunting career. Choices.

The Jews in Jesus' day had to make choices as well. And these choices were much more important than sticking an arrow in a deer. Jesus rocked the Jewish community with his teachings. For generations, the Jews had been taught to adhere to the law that God gave to them. Then along comes the son of a carpenter and tells them that he is coming to "fulfill" the law and that they could be free from it. The Jews, should they accept Christ, had to cut their tethers to the law and cleave to Christ. Big choices. And these choices were not easily made.

I can only imagine what that must have felt like to the Jews of that day. For generations, they had been correctly taught that they were the chosen people. They were well versed in scripture and history. They knew the story, and they thought they knew how it would end. A Messiah would ride into town and end the tyranny of the Roman Empire. He would rule and the Jewish people would come back with the power to control their own destiny. But instead, they received God's perfect son that came to free them from so much more than Roman tyranny. He came to free them from the truly tyrannical rule of sin in their lives. And so, the choice to tether themselves to this real Messiah meant that they would have to accept the fact that they were sinners and separate from God.

When Paul wrote to the Romans, he asked them to analyze their bondages. They could either be slaves to the world, which leads to destruction or be slaves to righteousness. He explains that you will be chained to something in this life. If they would choose to be tied to righteousness rather than worldliness, the final outcome would be vastly better.

What are you harnessed too? Are you a slave to the world or a slave to righteousness? Choose the latter, and you may see some of the "bucks" of this lifetime turn tail and run, but the benefits that you will reap will last far longer in eternal glory.

"But now you have been set free from sin and have become slaves to God, the benefit you reap leads to holiness and the result is eternal life."

Romans 6:22

23. The Camouflage

I must admit that I am part of the "problem". Hanging from my rear-view mirror is one of those little smelly trees. While it doesn't smell anything like a tree, it does reveal a little about the hearts of sportsmen. You see that little tree is camouflage. It's a nice, name-brand camo pattern. As if, when I was cruising through the woods, the deer will peek shyly out of the undergrowth and think, "Oh, I thought I heard a truck coming, but there is a tiny little tree in there. It must be OK." Give me a break. That camo pattern does nothing more than jack up the price of having a decent smelling truck. The list is a mile long. Camo cell phones. Camo trucks. Camo bed sheets. Camo lingerie. If it can be made and a hunter might see it, they slap camo on it.

The "problem" I am talking about can be demonstrated in slightly more subtle ways as well. I live in Montana and it is the accepted norm that if you possess an X and a Y chromosome you also possess a hunting rifle. Men are supposed to hunt. It's our culture. Now, I am under no allusions. Not all men hunt. There are some that don't choose to hunt, but don't want to be marginalized in our western society. Call them "posers" if you will. They have the big trucks (possibly with camo seat covers). They have the right clothes. But they don't have that killing edge. You see them everywhere. Decked out in some fashionable khaki slacks with a short-sleeved shooting shirt on. And of course, that extra thick patch on the shoulder is camo. Those clothes have never been off the pavement, unless the road to the country club is quaint gravel.

My camo is in rough shape. I can't afford to replace it every year, so it gets a little tattered and hopefully stained. I have one set of retired camo that I hunted in for over half of a hunting season with no crotch in the pants. Early one September I was climbing up my steps into a treestand in the pre-dawn light. As I hoisted my leg up, I heard an ominous rip. I continued up to my stand and then surveyed the damage. It was severe, front to back entirely gone. It was at that point that I wished I joined the posers in my purchasing of camo undergarments. I hunted the rest of the day and with some iron-on patches I finished out the season.

Jesus taught against the posers of his day as well. They weren't parading around with camo cell phones, but they did make a scene at the synagogues. "Righteous" men would come waltzing in with much fanfare and announce that they were giving a large sum to the needy. It was the social equivalent of pumping gas into their gold-plated SUV while wearing camo. Their gift wasn't truly meant for the purpose of helping the needy, but for gaining the appreciation of their peers. It wasn't that giving to the needy was wrong, but the motive in their hearts was not what Christ was after. The next time you pull on your favorite set of camo, I hope it is beat up and stained from years of good use. I also hope that the only things that see you dressing up like a tree are the trees themselves. And it is God's hope that as you work to further the kingdom and give to those in your society that are needy that He is the only one that sees it. After all, His eyes are the only ones that count.

"So when you give to the needy, do not announce it with trumpets, as the hypocrites do in the synagogues and on the streets, to be honored by men. I tell you the truth, they have received their reward in full. But when you give to the needy, do not let your left hand know what your right hand is doing, so that your giving may be in secret. Then your Father, who sees what is done in secret, will reward you."
Matthew 6:2-4

24. The First Knife

Deep in my heart, I knew that the "Bambi" moment was unfolding before my eyes. My three-year-old son, Carson, was admiring the antlers of a four by four whitetail with split brow tines that I had just drug down to the truck. It was cold and I had taken off my sweatshirt and draped it over him. He even had on my wool gloves. Seeing my deer had him chattering excitedly. All of a sudden, his big brown eyes welled up with tears. And then came the serious crying. He was almost inconsolable. I didn't want to ask him the question, but I knew I must.

"What's the matter, buddy?"

Through sobs and snorts came his reply, "I don't . . . have a sharp knife. . . to take the guts out with."

Oh, what elation on my part! I scooped up the boy and promised him that he could help me with my sharp knife. We would surely get the guts out. A few days later, Carson stood on a kitchen chair and helped me butcher that deer. In his hand he held a little paring knife that was probably less effective than the butter knives that he refused as "not sharp enough". But for three hours he toiled with me, turning a few little chunks of meat into well-loved burger meat.

Two years later I stopped with both of my boys at a little garage sale that had advertised "huntin stuff" on a piece of cardboard taped to a stop sign. There wasn't much at the sale that caught my eye as I took the obligatory laps around the tables. I turned to see Carson hovering at one particular corner of a wobbly folding table. The man putting on the sale noticed him too. As I approached him, I saw a rusty, dirty lock blade knife with a wood grip and brass ends in my son's hand. He turned it over and over pondering the possibilities. The man leaned over to my son and said the most beautiful words to a five-year-old's ears, "You can just take that if your dad says it's OK."

Carson's head snapped around locking on my eyes, his stare burning into my mind and melting my heart. He didn't even say a word.

"It's OK, tell the man thank you."

At that moment, holding a greasy little lock-blade that had probably been lost in the bottom of a tackle box, my son became a man. He had a knife; a real knife, a sharp knife. I think he was a bit taller as he strode with that prize squeezed tightly in his hand.

The quiet ride home was punctuated with an odd question.

"Dad, what hunting season is it?"

"It's not really any season right now. Bear season starts next week. I guess you could shoot a coyote."

"Well, dad, if we see a coyote on the way home, and you shoot him," he paused to sit up a little straighter in his car seat, "I will take the guts out with my sharp knife."

I'm sure you will buddy. I'm sure you will.

There is nothing quite like watching our children grow up. Our hopes and prayers for them are that they will desire to know and serve Christ as much as my son wanted that knife. "Like newborn babies, crave pure spiritual milk, so that by it you may grow up in your salvation, now that you have tasted and seen that the Lord is good." (I Peter 2:2-3) We are to crave the goodness of the Lord. I'm not sure that if someone were to describe my desire for the Lord, that they would use the term "crave". I'm afraid they might use terms like, "he admires the Lord", or "he likes the Lord", maybe even "loves the Lord". But to crave is something altogether different. We are to hover around the corner of the wobbly folding table of the Lord so that even a complete stranger feels the passion and desire coming from your being. That is craving.

I'm sure the next time I let a perfect arrow go, I will hear a little click behind me. It will be a boy with a greasy little lock blade. Ready to take out the guts. He knows what he has, and he knows how to use it.

"God said through the prophet, Jeremiah, "Then you will call upon me and come and pray to me, and I will listen to you. You will seek me and find me when you seek me with all your heart."
Jeremiah 29:12-13

25. Tuning Your Cams

My dad still has his first compound bow. I don't know what brand it is because the owner before my dad had spray-painted a camo pattern over the wooden limbs. There are two tiny little cams which offer a pitiful amount of let-off, when compared to today's 80%. One of the hardest parts about tuning those old compounds was dealing with the timing. Both the top and bottom cams had to be synched perfectly in order to get good arrow flight. And good arrow flight is what bow hunting is all about.

If one cam turned over even a fraction before the other, unequal forces would be applied to the string and would torque the arrow as it was propelled off of the rest. It is that perfect unity in cam action that allowed that bow to shoot well. And it did shoot well. I still remember when I was five years old, watching my dad wade through a stream chasing down a five by five mule deer with his hand-painted bow in hand. I didn't actually get to see him shoot it, but I have always had the antlers from his first bow-kill in my room. Both cams working together produce a fine product.

In scripture, James dealt with unity of two different forces. He looked at how to time the "cams" in our life; faith and deeds. Through our own personalities and choices we can often find one or the other of these two to be easier. At times it is easy to sit in our room and have faith in Christ. At other times it can be easy to put our heads down and plow through our daily work without paying any attention to the encouragements of the Holy Spirit. But our faith must be demonstrated to the unbelieving world by our deeds.

Our church was broken in to and vandalized by three teen-aged boys. They ruined lots of equipment and were looking to steal anything of worth. They were caught in the act and sent over to juvenile detention. That next Sunday, our pastor challenged us to put our faith into action. What would Christ have us do in this situation? Our flesh told us that they should have to pay for all of the damage. But Christ, through our faith, told us to bless those young men. So that very Sunday, an offering was taken. I was amazed to see a congregation walking down the aisles and filling three plastic tubs with money and literally the coats off their back. That money was used to buy gift boxes for each of the perpetrators. There were X-boxes, iPods, gadgets and toys delivered to each of them. The national media found out the actions of our church and our pastor and his wife were able to go on national television and explain that faith without deeds doesn't mean anything. Now, almost a year later, one of those young men has given his heart to the Lord and attends our church!

James encourages us to get our cams in time with each other. Faith and deeds must work together to provide a good witness. Check you cams today and make sure that your faith cam is timed perfectly with your deeds cam. What you believe and what you do must work together.

"Show me your faith without deeds, and I will show you my faith by what I do."

James 2:18

26. The Game Ear

I felt stupid pretending to be a deer in my hunting partner's back yard. Mark had gone down to the discount mega-store and bought a cheap sound amplifier similar to a Walker's Game Ear. So in the dark, he convinced me to try to sneak up on him in his back yard which I was actually able to do pretty easily. When testing the earpiece, he said the wind, his own breathing, and the kids running around in the house overwhelmed him. So he humbled himself, ate the $14.99 and gave it to his 3-year-old son. I have yet to humble myself to the point that I think I need a Game Ear. I am young so I automatically assume that I am hearing everything that God intended for me to hear. My hunting partner might not agree.

A few years ago we were bowhunting in a new area, looking for places to hang stands. We had put our bows aside and sat down to eat a snack and survey the field and tree line. We sat there for 10 minutes listening to an annoying little bird flitter around a large bush. While it kept my adrenaline flowing, I had a hard time convincing myself that a deer would feed on that bush 15 yards away for 10 minutes. As we left, so did the "bird" which was actually a fat doe that had been enjoying her time just a chip-shot away. I felt utterly foolish that we did not check it out! Realizing that your ears aren't hearing and understanding everything is truly a humbling experience.

One of the most overlooked experiences in the Christian walk is fasting. God called man to fasting. In scripture, the term "fasting" is often associated with the words "humble yourself". As we look back through our heavenly quiver, we find that a humble heart is actually our "anchor point". We all know that our anchor point is a highly important part of each shot. We also know that having a humble and contrite heart is highly important. So what about fasting? I will suggest two ways that fasting improves our Christian lives.

First, fasting takes the focus off of our physical bodies and puts it on our relationship with God. Not unlike a Game Ear, the act of removing the physical motion from our lives lets us perceive the spiritual moving more clearly. It is these small whispers of the Holy Spirit that often stay "on the other side of the bush". Most often, God uses a still small voice. Anything that we can do to humble ourselves and magnify Christ is highly valuable in our Christian walk.

Secondly, scripture points out that fasting also allows us to perceive what is going on around us in a physical sense as well. God describes these consequences of true fasting in Isaiah 58:6-9.

Is not this the kind of fasting I have chosen:
to loose the chains of injustice

and untie the cords of the yoke,
to set the oppressed free and break every yoke?
Is it not to share your food with the hungry
And to provide the poor wanderer with shelter-
When you see the naked, to cloth him,
And not to turn away from your own flesh and blood?
Then your light will break forth like the dawn,
And your healing will quickly appear;
Then your righteousness will go before you,
And the glory of the Lord will be your rear guard.
Then you will call, and the Lord will answer;
You will cry for help, and he will say: Here am I.

There are two types of magnification going on here. We are allowed to more clearly hear the will of God and we can see the physical and spiritual needs of those around us; all with renewed clarity. I can't wait for a Game Ear that can do that! Not only will I hear what is crunching through those leaves approaching my stand, but I will know their plans as well! This "Game Ear" is already accessible to those of us who are in Christ Jesus.

"You will cry for help, and he will say: Here am I."
Isaiah 58:9b

27. Practice, Practice, Practice

My teenaged legs were shaking as I eased up to the edge of the logging road; arrow nocked, release ready, mind spinning. I had just seen a fat mule deer doe come down off of the hillside and dump off below the road, out of sight. I eased up to peek over the edge, and there she was, broadside at 25 yards standing on a talus slope, with nothing to hide behind. It was perfect for my first bow kill. I came to full draw, held down on her vitals and touched off the arrow. It exploded in a loud crash on the rocks right beneath her. What? I couldn't believe it! I knew I could shoot that far, I practice that shot over and over in my back yard. Fortunately she behaved like a typical mule deer; bounded a couple of times and turned around to see what had happened. I'm not going to miss another broadside shot.

I sent my second arrow flying. The shot ended just like the first, in a clattering mess of carbon fiber and dust, right below her vitals. I watched as she got smart and left. I was kicking myself for my display of ineptitude. It was at that moment of ultimate questioning that I looked down at two little lines filed into the side of my sight. One mark was for broadheads and the other for field tips. You guessed it! My sight was set for field tips. I was disgusted. I had done everything right during the shot, but had neglected to take two seconds and an Allen wrench to prepare myself as I left the house.

You have heard the trite term "buck fever" over and over. And yes, I have struggled with it too. There is just no such thing as perfect practice in archery. In high school, I spent countless hours shooting into a spray painted deer target in my back yard. I would even stalk it on my hands and knees. I would creep up to a tree, come to full draw, lean around in the most awkward position, and smoke that target every time. There just isn't anything like the real thing.

Spiritually, there is one real thing. We are all guilty of sin and the penalty for our sin was paid by the sacrifice of Jesus Christ at Calvary. For generations before that, God had mandated the blood sacrifice of animals as an atoning act. But no number of dead bulls could clean away the stains of generations to come. The religious authorities were just practicing in the "back yard". Yes, it had to be done. God required it. Just like you and I spend time shooting in the off-season. It has to be done. But Christ didn't come to mess around in our back yard. He came once for all. No buck fever at Calvary. He faced the ultimate sacrifice of himself and touched off the perfect arrow; the arrow that will last for eternity.

"Day after day every priest stands and performs his religious duties; again and again he offers the same sacrifices, which can never take away sins. But when this priest [Jesus Christ] had offered for all time one sacrifice for sins, he sat down at the right hand of God."
Hebrew 10:11-12

28. The Small Peep

I remember the first time I had a peep sight installed on my compound bow. I was in high school and had scraped together enough money to buy the bow from a buddy. Any money I spent, I wanted to make the most of. So as I stood at the display with many different peep sights, I was searching for just the right one. The one I settled on was a variable peep. It had a small piece of plastic with holes drilled in it that got consecutively smaller. The concept being that in bright light conditions you could dial up the smallest and most specific hole. And when the light was fading, you could back it off to a much larger hole. That peep is still on that bow, although the bow has been retired to be my back-up bowfishing bow.

Do we live our lives like my dial peep? When the times are good and there is plenty of light to go around, it is easy to look through that tiny peep that points to the Lord. We can see Him clearly, and in focus; and see the things the Lord is doing for us. This is great and is a good way to live. However, we also have times that are not as bright. Life will bring trials, tests and troubles. There will be times that the world looks like those last couple of minutes of shooting light. You know the ones. When you are sitting in your stand squinting and hoping that the buck will come wandering by with just enough light to see. You glance anxiously at your watch as the seconds tick away towards the end of shooting hours. And should that buck come lumbering down the trail, if you did look through your tiny peep you might only see a dark smudge and not be able to focus.

This happened to me as I was trying to fill a doe tag early in my bowhunting career. I could see the fat doe just fine until I peeked through that tiny peep. Even with the dial pulled all the way out, it was still too dark. It was at this point that I made an ethical error. I held my eye just to the side of the peep, looking past it and not through it and let an arrow fly. Of course, it sailed off to the side and I missed completely.

I have felt myself wanting to do this in my life as well. When times are tough, it is so easy to take my eye away from that tiny peep that points to Truth and see if there is a better option on the outside. When we begin to make this search for more light, it leads us to break our form. No longer are we reaching the right anchor point. No longer are we lining up the string with our sights. We have fallen from God's perfect will for us.

Job experienced an incredible dark time in his life. Most of you would agree. Losing his family, his position in society, his wealth and his health are what most of us would see as just cause for being angry with God. But after his ranting and discussion with God he comes to this conclusion in his poem, "My ears have heard you but now my eyes have seen you. Therefore I despise myself and repent in dust and ashes." (Job 42:5-6) When was it that Job saw God? After his trials. Do you live your life content to have "heard of" the Lord? What will it take to force you to look through that tiny peep, ignoring the swirling circumstances and truly see the Lord?

Keep your eye focused through that tiny peep. There is only one way to heaven and you will never ever find it by lifting your head away from the peep. God built that sight just for you. Trust it.

"Enter through the narrow gate. For wide is the gate and broad is the road that leads to destruction, and many enter through it. But small is the gate and narrow the road that leads to life, and only a few find it."
Matthew 7:13-14

29. The Fall-away Rest

I have always loved the outdoors. My dad and I have spent many great days in the field. I started hunting with him when I was very young. My dad is always ready to tell the story of one of his favorite bowhunts when I was about four years old. As we were moving through the timber, my dad spotted a buck cutting across a slope above us.

I remember crouching down in my little gray sweatshirt and watching the buck, with his heavy rack cut across a scree slope. Knowing that I wouldn't be able to follow where he was headed, he sat me down next to a tree and told me not to move. My heart pounded as I crouched next to the pine with the rich smell of its needles mingling with the adrenaline that coursed through my body. As he circled up around the deer, he could constantly keep an eye on my location. While I know that some people in today's society might frown on this type of "neglect", it illustrates a beautiful point about our spiritual lives.

As we grow up in the Lord, whether that starts at a young age or much later in life, there is a time that we must be supported by strong mature Christians. I liken this to a fall away arrow rest. As the arrow is drawn back, the supporting arm cradles it. The rest lifts the arrow off of the shelf and points the broadhead straight toward the target. The potential energy in the limbs builds as the arrow reaches full draw. For a split second there is moment of anticipation, and then the arrow is cut loose. The rest waits until the arrow is moving and then drops away. No longer is there support on the bottom of the arrow, but yet it goes to the exact target it was just pointing at while fully supported.

We need to be given Christian love and support as we grow in Christ. We need the rest to point us to the target. Without the support, we are free to flop around in our faith and point to who-knows-where. Any of us who have accidentally shot an arrow off of the shelf know how this turns out. The arrow flies away in the wrong direction with a loud clang and wobbly flight. You need support.

The other side of the coin is when we find ourselves hanging on to the rest. An arrow does absolutely no good sitting on the rest. Even at full draw, which is the ultimate time of tension and anticipation, if you don't fly, you don't work. One of the first times I sat in a tree stand I got to experience full draw. I was set up on a well-used travel corridor in a small cluster of ponderosas. Two nice four by four whitetails, fresh out of velvet, stepped out onto my trail. The first buck walked behind the tree and I drew. But as I did, my elbow brushed the bark on the tree behind me. The buck froze. All I could see was his hind end sticking out from behind the tree a mere 13 yards from my stand. I held full draw for as long as I could, my arrow ready for action. My strength abandoned me and I let down. The buck slowly flipped a U-turn and left, never offering a good shot. I keep most of my bloody arrows as souvenirs. But the arrow that was on that rest that evening isn't in my collection. I don't even know which one it is. It didn't make an impact. To make an impact in life, you must fly.

My dad knew, when I was very young, when I was ready to be cut loose. As I sat next to the tree at four years old, I felt like a mountain man, lost in the wilderness. I wasn't flying though. My dad was still there pointing me. Now as I have my own family and have moved away, I am flying. It's not that I forget or abandon the teaching and support he put into me, I just know it's time for action. I am flying, right where he and many others pointed me.

"It was he who gave some to be apostles, some to be prophets, some to be evangelists, and some to be pastors and teachers, to prepare God's people for works of service, so that the body of Christ may be built up until we all reach unity in the faith and in the knowledge of the Son of God and become mature, attaining to the whole measure of the fullness of Christ."
Ephesians 4:11-13

30. The Sharp Knife

I'm not sure what men with knives have against arm hair, but there must be something because every time we test to see if our new knife is sharp, we hack away at that little patch of hair on the back our forearms. The quality of a knife's edge is measured in a few strokes down the back of my arm. If I shave a funny-looking bald patch into the back of my arm, at least I can feel confident that I have a sharp knife. In high school I worked at a fish hatchery. There were days when the older workers would take the tanker out and go plant fish and the other younger man and I were left to tidy up around the shop. Once the shop looked good, it was time to sharpen tools. We sharpened everything. There wasn't a shovel, hoe, rake, trowel, chisel, blade, or hammer that couldn't shave hair.

We also blazed a trail. Leading around the settling pond was an overgrown trail that had once been maintained. The kid and I decided to restore that path. We had an entire shop of razor sharp tools and put them to good use. We hacked, dug and widened our way around the pond. It was near the end of our workday that I came upon a stubborn branch. I had been hacking at it with some sort of sharpened implement. It didn't really matter what tool I was using, they had, at one time, all been "bald patch on the arm" sharp. But it was late in the day and the edge had worn off whichever tool I was using. I decided just to horse on the branch and see it I could break it. So with all my strength I heaved back on the branch. It exploded right in my hands sending a little chunk slicing right under my jaw. Picking my dazed self off the ground I grabbed my throat with a little ooze of blood forming between my fingers. To this day, I still blame dull tools for that scar on my chin.

In order to be effective, tools must be sharp. It works that way with hunting knives and it works that way with our spiritual lives as well. We all, at some time in our Christian life, will be a teacher. We may not have a classroom full of students taking notes, but someone is "taking notes" every time we open our mouth. When it comes time to teach your children about the ways of the Lord, or minister to that wayward neighbor, or encourage a grieving friend, we must be ready to point them straight to the Lord. We must be sharp.

Most of us have heard that a dull knife is actually more dangerous to the user than a sharp one. This is true when you teach as well. Your edge needs to be razor sharp and always pointing towards Christ. It is when we dull our edge with too much of ourselves that we become destined to harm. We are given opportunities daily to proclaim "self" or to proclaim "Christ". Our society and my stubborn heart say the same thing, "If you acknowledge Christ you might be weak." What a lie! My acknowledgment of dependence on Christ demonstrates my understanding of a complex universe. God created perfectly. He gave us free will. We chose self over God, and therefore sin was born. My dependence on the Savior only exclaims my ability to humble myself and fall into step with the all-powerful God of the universe. Am I weak? Absolutely. Am I willing to let God work? The answer to the second question will demonstrate my wisdom over my strength. We don't have to do all of the sharpening ourselves, however. Open yourself up to the workings of the Holy Spirit and watch as he puts an edge back on you. Sharpen yourself with the Word. Spend time with Knife Maker that created you. Make sure that when you go to teach the things of the Lord, you are ready to lay down some arm hair.

"You must teach what is in accord with sound doctrine."

Titus 2:1

31. The Full Quiver

This moment had been six years in the making. I had my longbow in hand and was closing the distance on a huge herd of bighorn sheep. Ever since I made my longbow in a dark, damp garage in Oregon, I had been dreaming about the moment that I would arrow my first animal with it. I had spent the whole summer practicing with my bow. I would go into the woods with my son in a backpack and we would romp through the trees sticking arrows in pinecones. It was only two weeks before my much-anticipated sheep season began, that my beloved bow exploded. After all of the preparation time I had put in, I was staring at a broken pile of fiberglass and walnut. After a little scrounging, I borrowed a longbow from a friend, retrained my eye to his bow, and was belly-crawling through the brush.

The sheep were working their way off of a flat and up a scree slope, nibbling on the brush as they went. I had been pinned down for 10 minutes as I watched them slowly file past at fifty yards, finally the last ewe went behind the line of trees and I began to close the distance. Staying on my belly, I figured that I could get to the tree line and be 20 yards right below where the sheep were feeding up in the rocks. And after crawling a couple hundred yards, my plan was almost complete. I say almost, because the last line of trees separating the sheep from my arrow, was incredibly thick. My backpack and quiver kept getting snagged and making noise. It was at that point I made a decision. I looked at my full quiver, pulled out a single arrow, and left everything but stick and string behind. I crawled through the tangle of brush and stood up behind the last tree.

The sheep had no idea I was there. There were two mature ewes and a young ram stripping a little bush about 25 yards away. I waited until the biggest ewe was quartering away, drew my lone arrow, found my anchor point and released. I watched in disbelief as the arrow sailed right beneath her brisket. The clattering arrow caused the whole herd to look around in confusion. They still had no idea what happened. But now I was left with a bow and no more arrows. I couldn't believe it; I had just blown my one opportunity.

In a last ditch effort, I turned away from the sheep and crawled back to my pack. I figured by the time I returned, the sheep would have scaled the impossible cliffs above me and be out of reach. I slid my pack back on and crawled again to the same pine tree, the branches ripping at my quiver. As I came through the line of brush, I saw the improbable. The sheep had returned!

I slipped another arrow out of the quiver and prepared to take the same shot I had just missed. As I was taking my last step around the tree, another ewe popped out onto the trail below me. 18 yards away was the culmination of my 6-year quest. Draw, anchor, release. My heart stopped as I watched the arrow blow through the sheep and stick into a tree on the other side. She took three bounds up the rock face as the herd scattered and then she fell and came to rest ten yards away.

A European mounted sheep is looking over my shoulder as I write this. That trophy wouldn't be there without a full quiver. But there are more important "trophies" in my life.

Every day I walk into a classroom of children to teach them about the world. Every day I walk down the street and avoid eye contact with people that I don't want to talk to. Every day, God gives me an opportunity to further His kingdom. And here is the kicker; He has equipped me to do it. Better yet, He has equipped you to do it. God doesn't leave us standing behind the last tree watching helplessly as our last arrow sails inches low.

I know that I often feel inadequate to do the will of my Father, but as I read in the closing prayer to the Hebrews, I am reminded of what I have been given. "May the God of Peace, who through the blood of the eternal covenant brought back from the dead our Lord Jesus, that great Shepherd of the sheep, equip you with everything good for doing his will, and may he work in us what is pleasing to him, through Jesus Christ, to whom be glory forever and ever. Amen." (Hebrews 13:20-21) Read that prayer again. It doesn't say that the Father will give us a little of what we need, or even most of it. The cry of Paul's heart was for the Hebrews, and now you and I, to receive everything that we need. A full quiver. God has put you on a path that will lead you to unspeakable trophies in your life. Realize where you are going, what you are shooting for, and then have the confidence to glance over your shoulder and see a quiver that is completely full.

"All scripture is God-breathed and is useful for teaching, rebuking, correcting and training in righteousness so that the man of God may be thoroughly equipped for every good work."
II Timothy 3:16-17

About The Author

Living with his family in Missoula, Montana, Brennan Koch has been given a great opportunity to pursue his outdoor passion. Brennan gets to share his experiences with his wife Jolene, and their two boys, Carson and Cooper.

Brennan was raised at a Quaker church camp in the mountains of central Idaho, where his passion for the outdoors was founded. He attended George Fox University where he met his wife. After receiving his Master's Degree in Teaching, he and his wife moved to Missoula to start a family.

Brennan is currently the chemistry teacher and athletic director at Valley Christian School where he is proud to be able to share his love of creation and the true heart of the Creator.

Visit our website for information, links to our video, as well as additional ordering opportunities.

www.thefullquiverbook.com

Made in the USA
San Bernardino, CA
31 January 2015